D1236166

Oral History

for the Local Historical Society

Second Edition, revised

by Willa K. Baum

American Association for State and Local History
Nashville, Tennessee,
by special arrangement with
The Conference of California Historical Societies

D16
B3
1977+

COPYRIGHT © 1969, 1971
BY WILLA K. BAUM
Printed in the United States of America

First Edition published 1969
Second Edition, 1971
Second Printing, Second Edition, 1972
Third Printing, Second Edition, brought up to date and corrected, 1974
Fourth Printing, Revised Second Edition, 1975
Fifth Printing, Revised Second Edition, 1977

FOREWORD

Two years ago the Conference of California Historical Societies published the first edition of Willa Baum's *Oral History for the Local Historical Society*. The booklet was an immediate critical success because of the expertise of its nationally recognized author and her ability to discuss a somewhat technical subject in easily understood terms. It was also a commercial success because it answered so well a growing need of local historical societies for help in establishing oral history programs.

When the initial printing of the booklet was nearly gone, the American Association for State and Local History made special arrangements to become the publisher of the second edition. We felt that the booklet deserved the widest possible distribution among our member organizations. Oral history is an increasingly important means of assembling information for historical research, particularly at the local level. It can be done by societies with limited resources, but its value to our knowledge of the past depends on its being done right. Mrs. Baum's booklet provides the guidance that is needed.

This new edition contains important revisions of the first publication. It has been completely redesigned, provided with new photographic illustrations, and printed from new type. It also has been up-dated in its recommendations regarding equipment, particularly to reflect the rapid technological progress in development of cassette recorders. We are proud to be its publisher, and grateful to the Conference of California Historical Societies for its willingness to share the publication with other societies through the American Association for State and Local History.

William T. Alderson
Director

CONTENTS

NOTE ON AUTHOR: Willa K. Baum is director of the Regional Oral History Office,
a department of the Bancroft Library, University of California at Berkeley. The Office
is engaged in tape-recording the memoirs of persons who have contributed significantly
to the development of the West. Mrs. Baum is a member of the council of the Oral
History Association and belongs to the Western History Association and the Conference of California Historical Societies. She has participated in the programs of those
associations and has also addressed special historical groups on the subject of oral
history.

What Is Oral History

The way of life that was characteristic of an earlier America is rapidly disappearing, but there are persons still alive today who remember it vividly. It is unlikely that they will preserve their pioneer memories by writing memoirs, as historians would wish them to do, but many old-timers are willing to tell their stories and confide their reminiscences to tape recordings. Likewise the busy citizen immersed in economic, political, or civic activities today may be willing to set aside time to tape-record the whys and hows of his efforts in order to preserve a more current history of the community. While the individual recordings are sometimes fragmentary and highly personal, taken together they provide a fund of color, detail, and incident invaluable for future historical research.

Oral history is the tape-recording of reminiscences about which the narrator can speak from first-hand knowledge. Through pre-planned interviews, the information is captured in question and answer form by oral history interviewers. The interviewer must have some background knowledge of the subject and considerable social skill in knowing how to draw the narrator out. Oral history is not the tape-recording of speeches or other community events, although this should be another part of the historical society's collecting program.

Oral history interviews differ from journalistic or specific historical research interviews in that they are intended for use in the future by a wide variety of researchers; therefore their scope should be broader than what would be covered for immediate or specific use.

Why Oral History

Local historical societies have assumed the responsibility of preserving the history of their communities. In this effort they engage in collecting, preserving, and making available for research manuscripts relating to the community, such as diaries, letters, business and civic records. They preserve the implements and photographs of life in a bygone era and often establish museums so that these may be seen by the public. Historic sites are preserved or reconstructed, and maintained for public viewing. Through a publications program or a lecture program, the historical society stimulates historical research and the dissemination of the results of that research.

Oral history is a relatively new and increasingly essential part of the efforts of the local historical society. In this day of hurried contacts, telephone or face-to-face meetings, and multitudinous evening activities, people no longer write the long letters, the routinely kept diaries, the series of letters back and forth to work out an agreement, the careful memos that heretofore have always served as the bones of historical research. And, as always, there are many classes of persons who will not set down in writing the description of their way of life although they may have a very rich oral tradition and may be able to talk with much color and accuracy about this life.

These gaps can now be filled by oral history. Through the relatively painless medium of relaxed conversations based upon well-planned questions, it is possible to elicit information that would not ordinarily get into the written record: the descriptions of the appearance and character of leading citizens, the motivations as to why and how and by what "gentleman's agreement" things came to pass, the life and color of a community or an industry or an ethnic group.

In addition to providing research information,

oral history can serve as a link from the immediate present to the immediate past in an understandable and very human way that can give the young and the newcomers a way of sinking their roots into the community.

Most importantly, because local historical societies are manned by volunteer workers, oral history can be fun for the interviewer, the narrator, and anyone else concerned with the work.

How to Start an
Oral History Program

Set Up a Committee

Start with a small group of members of the historical society who have indicated an interest in collecting the history of this century. The number of your committee, their individual interests, and the time they have available for this work will indicate how extensive an oral history program you should plan.

Make Preliminary Plans:
Who Should Be Interviewed?

It is usually recommended that you organize a community survey by which you establish what the major community developments of interest have been, what recorded information on them already exists, what persons are available who can tell about these things, and then in what priority they should be interviewed. It has been my observation, however, that such a survey takes too long, that as a result part of your interested group will drop out before you are ready to begin interviewing, and that several of your prime prospective narrators will die or become incapacitated while you are considering.

At the risk of sounding unprofessional, I recommend that you immediately decide upon three or four persons to be interviewed who are known to the group for their first-hand knowledge of community developments, and that you begin the interviewing program without delay. At the same time, you may conduct the community survey. Your whole program will develop and change as you go. Often the best sources of information on whom to interview will be your narrators themselves.

In deciding whom to start with, take into consideration factors of age and health. Actuarial statistics will give some of your prospective narrators only a slim chance of being here next year. Don't be afraid to start with them. If you do a poor job due to inexperience, wait six months, and then go back and do the interviews over if the narrator is still able. If he isn't, console yourself that a poor interview is better than none.

At the same time as you are beginning the interviewing program, you can be preparing a list of topics to be covered in the interviews, and a list of additional potential narrators. A brief notice in the local paper to the effect that the society is gathering information on "the history of Valley County since 1910," or "the history of the schools in Valley County since 1910," and that you would appreciate having the names of persons who might be able to tell about that subject, will give you some leads.

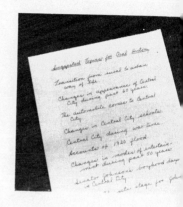

Do not indicate that you intend to interview these persons on tape, either in a newspaper account or in a preliminary letter or by any other way. You will soon have far too many names, so do not commit yourself until you have had a chance to evaluate the prospective narrator, and until you know how much work your committee can handle.

Consider a Questionnaire

It is often helpful to prepare a questionnaire which can be sent to all recommended narrators. This questionnaire when returned can be used to help you decide whom to call on personally; if you decide to interview the person, it can be the beginning of an outline for this interview. The questionnaire must be designed to fit your own topics.

Here is a sample questionnaire which proved very useful to a volunteer oral history committee working on the history of a college women's society. In keeping with a policy of getting the oldest first, the questionnaire was sent to all pre-1920 alumnae, and from the answers a list of narrators was prepared.

PRYTANEAN SOCIETY ORAL HISTORY QUESTIONNAIRE

Name _____ Class _____

Maiden Name _____ No. of Children _____

Address _____ Phone_____

Birthplace _____

Why did you go to the University of California? _____
_____

What was your major? _____

What were your extra-curricular activities? _____
_____

What were some of the things that Prytanean did while you were on campus? _____
_____
_____
_____

Did you prepare yourself for a profession? _____

If so, which one? _____

Did you actually work in this profession (or some other)? _____

Please give brief details _____

Do you feel that your college work helped to prepare you for the life you have
actually lived? _____

How would you have changed your preparation if you could have looked into the
future? _____
_____

List some of your most significant "extracurricular" or civic activities since graduation
_____
_____
_____

What has been your participation in Prytanean Alumnae affairs? _____
_____
_____

What has been your participation in University Alumni affairs? _____
_____

☐ I should be glad to have a volunteer interviewer talk with me about my recollec-
tions of the Prytanean Society.

I am available except as noted below:

Prepare a General List of Questions

The outline for every person's interview will have to be prepared separately and should be based on that person's career or his vantage point in the events you are inquiring about. However, there will be general questions that you will ask all the narrators—some biographical, some topical.

Biographically, you will want to establish the individual's identity. Depending on your purposes, this may be answered in five minutes or in one or two interviews. The questions should include father's and mother's names and a little on their background, such as where they came from, and something about their occupations. For genealogical purposes, more information on the family tree may be sought. (Since this is hard to keep track of verbally and takes much time, the narrator might be willing to prepare a family chart in writing to be added to his file.) Then, of course, the narrator's birthdate and birthplace, his education, travels, occupation, spouse and children.

Topically, there will be major national and community events you will ask about—the effect of World War I, the Depression, the San Francisco Earthquake, certain strikes, the Bank Holiday, etc. Good general references for this kind of information are college history textbooks and your own state, county, and city histories.

From these, and from histories of the topics you may be investigating (i.e., livestock, mining, seafaring), you should be able to draw up a general list of important events to ask about. From there on, it is the responsibility of each interviewer to tailor-make the interview outlines to his individual narrators.

Print Stationery or Calling Cards

It should always be clear to the persons from whom you collect historical materials that this is a historical society endeavor, not an individual endeavor, even though the oral history committee

Jane Doe

Oral History Committee

CAN ASSOCIATION FOR STATE AND LOCAL HISTORY
th Avenue South · Nashville, Tennessee 37203 · Telephone [615] 242-5583

may be a committee of one. Persons you deal with should have in writing the name of the society and of the person they are talking to.

Most historical societies have letterhead stationery already printed, and this should be used for all official communications about interviews. If there is no stationery, the oral history committee should have some printed. If the program will be a substantial one with many contacts with the public, calling cards should be printed, identifying the historical society and providing a blank area that each member of the committee can use to fill in his own name. This card should be given to persons you call on in person for information or for historical papers; a confirming letter on historical society letterhead should follow.

Equipment and Tapes

One of the nice things about oral history is that the equipment required is so inexpensive and so readily available. Cost for a tape recorder plus tapes will be under $300, under $150 in some instances. Special transcribing equipment will cost more, but it is not necessary in the beginning. Plan to buy your equipment at a local electronics shop which has a reputation for standing behind its products, and for handling repairs competently.

Tape Recorders

If you appoint a committee to select a tape recorder, you will naturally put on it your most knowledgeable person on electronics. Be sure also to include on the committee several persons who will be using the recorder but who have no mechanical talents. The recorder chosen must be one they will be comfortable with, as well as one that is satisfactory to the high-fidelity buff.

There are a number of suitable tape recorders on the market, and models change so quickly that it is difficult to recommend any special one. Consult your local electronics dealer, keeping in mind the following considerations:

1. Ease of operation
2. Portability and weight
3. Reliability of recording: Is the recorder recording?
4. Adequacy of the sound: Can the voices be heard and understood without interference from much machine noise?

You should, if possible, get a machine that is convenient to carry and one that will operate on AC current and DC batteries as well. Always plan to use AC current when it is available to avoid the problems of uneven recording speed that come with fading batteries.

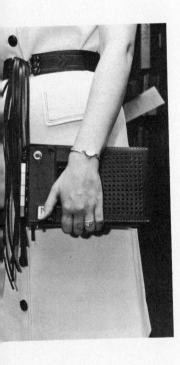

We have found automatic volume control to be very useful. This adjusts the volume automatically and instantly to record correctly a loud voice or a soft voice.

Test several machines for sound fidelity. The spoken word does not require the frequency range that music does. While you will want the best sound fidelity you can get for the money, this aim can conflict with that of ease of operation.

The machine should be dependable and have a low frequency-of-repair record. Be sure that repair service and parts are available if needed.

In my opinion, ease of operation is a paramount consideration. It is easy to be persuaded by the electronics dealer (who feels very comfortable around electronic equipment, else he would have gone into some other business) that making a few extra adjustments as you set up the recorder will not be beyond your capacity. What he will not realize is that you will have so many things to think about in starting an interview that you can forget one of those mechanical adjustments and lose your whole recording. So stay with the push-button machine on which your only adjustment is volume, and not even that if you get automatic volume control.

Up to now, reel-to-reel recorders have been the only reasonable choice, but because of new improvements cassette recorders are now feasible for oral history. There are advantages and disadvantages to each.

I. *Reel-to-Reel Recorders (1974 Prices)*. Reel-to-reel recorders offer better sound fidelity, greater control over the tape, and greater reliability in that, come what may, you will pobably end up with a recording. If the tape becomes tangled, the machine can be stopped and the tape untangled; if broken, it can be spliced, or, during the interview, just held in place for a turn or two, so that it will catch and go on. The splice can be made later. The turning of the reels and the approaching end of the tape are clearly visible so that you can plan ahead as to when to end the interview or when to turn the tape. Reel tape is wider than cassette tape, providing a greater area for the magnetic signal; reel recordings from equivalent microphones and machines will be slightly superior to those on cassettes.

One supposed advantage of reels over cassettes that is always mentioned by tape-recorder buffs is the possibility of editing the tapes by cutting, rearranging, and splicing. While this is something one would do if production of a well-put-together sound recording were your purpose, I feel it has no part in oral history. The original tape should not be cut or doctored up in any way. If a sound recording is desired to play on the radio, in a class or meeting, or for a civic celebration, a new tape, edited and rearranged, can be prepared by re-recording the desired portions from one tape to another. This can be done equally well from a reel or a cassette. Cutting up the original tape should have no part in the program nor in the consideration of types of tape recorders.

If you decide on reel-to-reel, plan to use 5-inch reels which can be played back on most machines. Standardize your recording at 3¾ ips (inches per second), a middle speed that all tape recorders handle (some also go at $1^{5}/_{16}$, $1^{7}/_{8}$, or $7^{1}/_{2}$).

The number of reel-to-reel machines available today in the under-$500 range is limited. Therefore, two heavier machines using AC current only are listed. The project may be able to buy one AC/DC cassette recorder to take care of interviews requiring battery operation or a small machine.

REALISTIC 505 A (Radio Shack, cat. no. 14-883)—AC/DC, about nine pounds, 5-inch reel, automatic volume control, external mike only. A fair machine and all there is at a modest price. $80.

SONY TC-800B—AC/DC, twelve pounds, 5-inch reels, automatic volume control, built-in mike and also external mike. An excellent machine with several extra features that are useful. $300.

SONY TC-106AV (audio-visual, available at stores handling educational supplies)—AC only, eighteen pounds, 7-inch reels, external mike only. An excellent machine except for weight, and that it requires house current. $200.

WOLLENSAK 1500SS—AC only, nineteen pounds, 7-inch reels, external mike only. A reliable machine that will take hard wear. $205.

2. *Cassette Tape Recorders (1974 Prices).* Cassette recorders offer many advantages to oral historians, the first and foremost being small size and ease of operation. Cassettes are small plastic cartridges which encase the narrow tape permanently. A cassette machine will weigh no more than five pounds and is a small and compact unit. Some come with built-in microphones so that nothing is required but to set the machine on the table and flip the switch (if you use battery and not current). It will record with no visible motion of the reels. The cassettes are simply dropped into place; there is no threading of the machine required. At the end of the tape (30 or 45 minutes), the cassette can be flipped over in a second and is ready to go again for another similar time period.

The cassette recorders with built-in mikes are especially convenient to use. However, a built-in mike can seldom get the sound fidelity of a remote mike; unless the machine is working perfectly, there will be some feedback or machine noise from the motor. The machines with built-in mikes come with remote mikes also. The interviewer can decide whether the better sound of the remote mike or the unobtrusiveness of the built-in mike is more important in each situation.

The cassette tapes offer excellent storage protection. They usually come in a plastic or paper box ready for labeling. An even greater joy to the oral historian is the fact that two little holes in the back of the cassette can be pushed out, after which the recording heads will no longer engage the tape. By doing this the tape can be played over and over but cannot be accidentally erased.

The cassette tapes, when first introduced, had several crucial disadvantages which have now been improved. They tended to tangle or jam, and being fully encased, there was nothing that could be done about them; in fact, since they turn almost invisibly, the operator might be unaware of the fact that no recording was going on. The new cassettes are more reliable, but still not foolproof—anyone using them should come prepared with a few extra cassettes to use in emergency. And don't buy off-brand cassettes; they are more likely to jam.

The second great problem was that there was almost no way to know when they came to the end. Unless he set an alarm clock to time the interview, the interviewer would either have to sit on pins and needles as the end time approached, or take a chance on missing a part of the interview. This problem has been lessened by end-alarm recorders and cassettes. These have a little metal strip at the end of the tape which activates a buzzer and thus sounds the end of the tape. Use end-alarm tapes if the recorder allows, or use a parking-meter buzzer set for the time of the tape.

As previously mentioned, the sound fidelity of cassette recorders is not quite up to reel-to-reel recorders, but those mentioned below are entirely adequate for the spoken voice. The list by no means includes all suitable machines.

HITACHI TRQ-340—AC/DC, 5 pounds, built-in mike (external mike can be purchased extra), automatic volume control. A back-space review button makes this useable as a transcribing machine. $90.

HITACHI TRQ-33—DC only (requires an adapter to use AC), only two pounds, built-in mike (external mike can be purchased extra). This machine lacks the review button and AC of the above Hitachi, and its small size means the play-back speaker is poor, but it is an excellent DC recording machine if very small size is important. $90.

SONY TC-90A—AC/DC, five pounds, built-in and external mikes, automatic volume control, back-space review button. An excellent machine, useable for transcribing. $100.

SONY TC-100A—AC/DC, four pounds, built-in and external mikes, back-space review button, end-of-tape alarm. The favorite machine for news reporters and many oral historians. $129.

Microphones

It is possible to purchase better-quality microphones that will give you better recordings. In keeping with my philosophy that the simpler you keep the technical part of the recording, the better, I do not recommend them to start with. After your program is well under way you may wish to consider a better microphone. Be sure you take your recorder with you when you try microphones. Mikes and recorders have to have matching impedances and matching plugs or they will not fit together.

We have obtained noticeably better sound through the use of lavalier mikes. These are small mikes which hang about the neck of the narrator or can be clipped to his lapel. They are particularly useful with a narrator who speaks with difficulty or for recording in a noisy place. An especially excellent lapel mike that fits any Sony machine is the Sony ECM-16 electroset condenser mike ($30). Because using two mikes (narrator and interviewer) requires a transistorized mike mixer, I suggest that the interviewer go without one and plan to speak up loudly enough to be picked up on the narrator's mike.

Tapes and Cassettes

1. *Reels.* Reels should be 5-inch polyester (nylon), low-noise. While it is sometimes possible to buy good-quality tape under a house brand name, unless you have a recommendation from a reliable electronics dealer, you had better stick to good-quality standard brands.

2. *Cassettes.* Cassettes should be low-noise, bolted cases, middle-price range for the brand (the highest price range is for recording sound frequencies that are not needed for speech). Do not buy off-brands or bargain cassettes, as the least malfunction of the cassette will cost you more than your bargain could save you. Bolted cases (screws in the four corners rather than the case fused together) give you some chance of opening and repairing a damaged cassette tape. You can buy empty cassette cases to use for replacements. Your electronics dealer may be able to repair what you can't. (As a very last resort, True Recording Company, 3883 Piedmont Avenue, Oakland, California 94611, will repair cassettes, if possible, for about $3 each, plus shipping.) Good tapes are Scotch (fused case but low damage record), Hitachi, and Maxell. Sony tapes have end-alarm, but tangle more.

Recording tape (reels and cassettes) comes in different thicknesses. The thinner the tape, the more time you can get per side. Also the more difficulties you may expect through damage to the tape in the stop/start action necessary to transcribing or listening in detail, and in print-through when the tape is stored.

Do not use 5-inch reels or cassettes that play more than 30 minutes or 45 minutes per side.

Recorder	Footage	Time per side at 3¾	Average cost of standard brands
Reels, 5-inch	600 ft.	30 min.	$2.30
	900 ft.	45 min.	$2.85
Cassettes C-60		30 min.	$2.50
C-90		45 min.	$3.75

Discounts are usually available if you buy in quantity.

Splicers

Whether you plan it that way or not, the time will come when you have a broken tape and will have to splice it. This can be done with a razor blade, tweezers, and a roll of splicing tape, but it will be very much easier if you buy a splicing machine. Splicing machines are available for reel and cassette tapes for under $5.

The Interview Process

Contacting the Narrator

Call or write the prospective narrator indicating that you are surveying sources of information on the history of the community (or whatever your theme may be) and would like to talk to him about this. Do not bring up the oral history aspect at this time. When you meet, inquire about his background and take notes on his biographical data; find out if he has or knows of papers or other materials of historical significance. In the course of the conversation, you will be getting the material you need to prepare interview outlines, and you will be able to evaluate him personally as a prospective narrator. Depending on your committee's plans, you may decide then and there to interview him, and immediately invite him to participate; or you may take the information back to the committee and use it as a basis for establishing a narrator list.

Explaining the Program to the Narrator

The invitation to participate can come personally or by letter. In either event, you should explain what the purpose is and how the interviewing will proceed. Answer questions such as: Where will the tapes be kept when the interviewing is finished? Who may use them and under what circumstances? May the narrator get a copy of the tape for himself? How many sessions do you plan? (Always start with far fewer sessions than you expect to do. It is easy to decide to do more as you proceed; it is almost impossible to lower the number of sessions you suggest originally.)

At the Bancroft Library we usually explain the project, then follow up with a letter reiterating the plan, and ask the narrator to sign and return a carbon copy of this letter if it meets his approval. We feel it helps to avoid misunderstandings if all parties concerned have a clear and permanent record of what they have agreed upon.

A Planning Session with the Narrator

Talk over with the narrator the subjects you will discuss in the course of the interviews. The biographical data he has already given you will be your first guideline. He may suggest topics he knows a lot about; you will ask him if he knows about others as well; plan together what you will include in the recordings.

A common problem in this planning session is to keep the conversation on what you *will* talk about, but without getting into the details right then. The information you will get on the tape will be much fresher and livelier if he hasn't told you the story already at the planning session. Avoiding this can be very difficult, and it is a good idea to plan a short session and inform your narrator ahead of time that you have an unbreakable appointment in an hour. For the very loquacious narrator you may need a definite time when you must leave after each interview.

Preparing Interview Outlines

At home you will prepare a very general outline of what you plan to talk about for the entire course of interviews, plus a more specific outline of the first interview. Keep this in brief outline form. *Do not* word the questions. For example: "Father's background—parents, school, occupation"; not, "What was your father's name? What was his occupation?" etc. An already-worded question will sound like a canned speech when you read it and will destroy the informality of your interview.

Most interviewees appreciate receiving a copy of the interview outline a few days before the session; for a few this is just a worry. Every step of the way you will have to adjust what you do to what works best with a specific narrator.

Remind the Narrator of the Interview Appointment

Whether you do or don't send an outline, do drop the narrator a line or telephone him a few days before the scheduled taping session just to remind him of the time, date, and topics you will be discussing. This will encourage him to refresh his memory by looking over his papers, talking to his spouse, or just ruminating.

Practice with the Tape Recorder Beforehand

If you are not thoroughly familiar with the tape recorder, practice at home setting it up and putting it away so this will not cause you any concern. Using your family or a friend as a foil, practice casually setting up the machine, including crawling under tables in search of electrical outlets while carrying on a conversation. Become proficient at it; you will have too many other things to think about at the time of the first interview to have to worry about the machine.

Plan a Formal Introduction to the Tape

Plan a formal introduction for the tape which gives the place and date, the narrator's name and briefly who he is, and who you are. For example: "This is an interview with John P. Kringle, retired banker of the Central City Trust Company of Central City. Mr. Kringle has been a banker since 1915, having worked through the World War I years, the agricultural depression of the 1920's, the Great Depression and the effects of the Bank Holiday, World War II, the land boom of the 1950's, and the absorption of the Central City Trust Company into the Bank of America in 1962. This interview is being conducted on April 17, 1969, at Mr. Kringle's home on East Hampton Street. The interviewer is William Smith, representing the Central City Historical Society."

Practice this introduction on the tape and determine how much tape it will take. If possible, set up your recorder with a blank lead of that much tape before you go, or be prepared to wind that much tape onto the take-up reel before you begin to record.

But do not record the introduction beforehand, or your narrator may hear it as you try the recording out. And positively do not record the introduction when you start the interview. There is nothing that can give your narrator mike-fright more surely than for you to speak a formal introduction and then let him know that he is "on the air." After you get home, you can read your introduction onto the blank tape you have left on the front of the reel.

Starting the Interview: Setting Up the Equipment

Arrive at the appointed time.

Situate the interview where there will be as few interruptions as possible. Discourage the presence of a third party, especially a husband or wife. (Interview them separately if they can add to the account.)

Be sure the narrator is comfortable. Don't let him give you his favorite chair.

After you have determined where you will sit, locate the recorder where you can see it but he cannot. (Of course you will have an extension cord along.) While he should know when you are recording, there is no need to concern him with the spinning of the reels or the flickering of the volume level light. Watching that is your job alone. A good place to put the recorder is on the floor near your chair (not on a rug if your machine is ventilated from the bottom); try to have a table or coffee table between you and the narrator, and place the mike on the table. Never put the recorder and the mike on the same table. Placing the mike on a folded scarf with one or two folds over the mike will help to deaden a few of the mechanical noises that fill the air and usually go unnoticed until they are preserved with amplified sharpness on your tape recording.

Establishing Rapport

Turn on the machine immediately and let it run while you chat a bit about the weather. Be relaxed, show no concern for the passage of tape. Your narrator may want to ask a few more questions. You may wish to remind him of the purpose of the recording. Tell him you will be taking notes on names and places and dates he mentions and you hope he will check the spelling after the interview. While you are chatting, casually rewind the tape and play it back, making sure the volume is adjusted to pick up his voice clearly and yours also. He will probably be interested in the sound of his voice on the tape and you can listen to a little of what you have recorded. Then go back to the point on the tape where you planned to begin.

Turn on the recorder, settle back, and slide into your first question easily. "Mr. Kringle, before we get into the early days of the Central City Trust Company, would you tell me something about yourself? Where and when were you born?"

Be interested. Listen to what your narrator is saying and make the appropriate comments. Do not be so concerned about your next question that when he stops for air, you blurt it out. He may not have finished what he was saying. This does not apply if he is very long-winded and you are trying to hustle him along into the next subject.

Taking Notes

Keep running notes on names, places, and dates he may mention. These will be of help to the person who listens to the tape at a later date and to you when you prepare an index of the tape. Most importantly, it will give you something to do during the long pauses when you do not want to stare silently into the narrator's eyes, nor want to speak before he has completed his thought. The most common error of the beginning interviewer is jumping into every silence with the next question. Taking notes will help prevent this, and will also

permit you to check spelling with your narrator at the close of the interview. Most narrators are flattered to think that you consider what they are saying important enough to be making notes.

Turning the Tape

Depending on the length of your tape, you will run out in 30 minutes, 45 minutes, or an hour. As this time approaches, keep one eye on the tape, and try to find a natural place to break before the tape runs out. If your narrator seems a little tired, this is the time either to suggest that you leave and come back next week, or that it will take you a few minutes to turn the tape and he is welcome to take a break.

If you turn the tape and continue after the break, slide into the topic again. "You were telling about the bank crash in '29. How did that affect your job?"

Closing the Interview

An hour and a half is usually maximum for an interview session. Although some narrators can go longer without fatigue, the interviewer usually cannot. One is often tempted to get just one more good story on the tape before turning off the recorder, but a few experiences of having the narrator (or his wife) call and cancel the next appointment because it is just too fatiguing will prove the folly of this plan.

Set the time limit in your own mind, then stop at an appropriate break in the story near that time. Explain you must be leaving shortly. Ask the narrator to check over the spelling of the names in your notes while you pack up the recorder. Spend a few minutes planning what you will discuss next time. Perhaps he will lend you a scrapbook or some mementos which will help you prepare the questions for next week. Try to leave no more than half an hour after the close of the recording; otherwise you will hear all the stories he is going to tell you next week.

Homework After the Interview

Shortly thereafter, prepare the tape for permanent record. Right after the interview it should have been labelled on the box, and on a label on the tape reel itself, with the name of narrator and interviewer, the date, the length of time of the recording, and the speed if you don't always use 3¾ ips. If this is a second or later interview, you should also indicate what number interview it is.

Record your introduction onto the lead-in tape at the front of the reel.

Having thus properly identified the tape, listen through it and prepare the tape index (see section on indexing). Note topics that need to be discussed further at the next recording session. Then listen through the tape again for your own training (see section on developing expertise).

Who Should Interview

As in any art, interviewing can be done in many ways by many different sorts of people, and although the results may be different, they can all be good. The very friendly, informal person will interview in one way; the more formal, correct, and controlled person will interview in another way. The interviewer should be someone who can sit quietly and listen, who is willing to let the narrator express an opinion contrary to his own without feeling compelled to contradict or re-educate the narrator, who is not afraid to break in occasionally with a question or guiding comment, who is firm enough to end the interview on time and to keep it within the bounds of whatever lines of inquiry have been planned, who is alert enough and knowledgeable enough to recognize when the narrator brings up an unplanned but valuable subject, and who is able to pursue that new subject with questions.

There are, however, two types of person who should not be assigned to interviewing. They are the compulsive talker, and the compulsive director. Both types will end up with interviews of themselves. The compulsive talker will do most of the talking, in the guise of lengthy questions or comments between brief yeses or noes of the narrator. The compulsive director will be able to guide the narrator into telling what the interviewer thinks is the appropriate account, much to the later dissatisfaction of the narrator and the non-validity of the historical information. So use the director-type to head up the program, and the talker-type to publicize the program, to raise funds for equipment, and to put the information that is obtained into use through lectures. Save the interviewing itself for the quieter people in the group.

A well-organized oral history program encompasses such a variety of activities that almost every personality type can make a satisfying contribution to the program. The very shy person who may feel uncomfortable interviewing may be ideal to keep the tape files organized, to index the tapes, to send information on the interviews to the state library, and to do transcribing if that is decided upon. The mechanically inclined may be prevailed upon to branch out and record other events such as major addresses or other important happenings. Ideally one member of the group will have the administrative skill to guide people into the right jobs for them.

Tips for Interviewers

1. An interview is not a dialogue. The whole point of the interview is to get the narrator to tell *his* story. Limit your own remarks to a few pleasantries to break the ice, then brief questions to guide him along. It is not necessary to give him the details of your great-grandmother's trip in a covered wagon in order to get him to tell you about his grandfather's trip to California. Just say, "I understand your grandfather came around the Horn to California. What did he tell you about the trip?"

2. Ask questions that require more of an answer than "yes" or "no." Start with "Why, How, Where, What kind of. . . ." Instead of "Was Henry Miller a good boss?" ask "What did the cowhands think of Henry Miller as a boss?"

3. Ask one question at a time. Sometimes interviewers ask a series of questions all at once. Probably the narrator will answer only the first or last one. You will catch this kind of questioning when you listen through the tape after the session and you can avoid it the next time.

4. Ask brief questions. We all know the irrepressible speech-maker who, when questions are called for at the end of a lecture, gets up and asks a five-minute question. It is unlikely that the narrator is so dull that it takes more than a sentence or two for him to understand the question.

5. Start with non-controversial questions; save the delicate questions, if there are any, until you have become better acquainted. A good place to begin is with the narrator's youth and background.

6. Don't let periods of silence fluster you. Give your narrator a chance to think of what he wants to add before you hustle him along with the next question. Relax, write a few words on your notepad. The sure sign of a beginning interviewer is a tape where every brief pause signals the next question.

7. Don't worry if your questions are not as beautifully phrased as you would like them to be for posterity. A few fumbled questions will help put your narrator at ease as he realizes that you are not perfect and he need not worry if he isn't either. It is unnecessary to practice fumbling a few questions; most of us are nervous enough to do that naturally.

8. Don't interrupt a good story because you have thought of a question, or because your narrator is straying from the planned outline. If the information is pertinent, let him go on, but jot down your question on your notepad so you will remember to ask it later.

9. If your narrator does stray into non-pertinent subjects (the most common problems are to follow some family member's children or to get into a series of family medical problems), try to pull him back as quickly as possible. "Before we move on, I'd like to find out how the closing of the mine in 1898 affected your family's finances. Do you remember that?"

10. It is often hard for a narrator to describe persons. An easy way to begin is to ask him to describe the person's appearance. From there, the narrator is more likely to move into character description.

11. Interviewing is one time when a negative approach is more effective than a positive one. Ask about the negative aspects of a situation. For example, in asking about a person, do not begin with a glowing description of him. "I know the mayor was a very generous and wise person. Did you find him so?" Few narrators will quarrel with a statement like that even though they may have found the mayor a disagreeable person. You will get a more lively answer if you start out in the negative. "Despite the mayor's reputation for good works, I hear he was a very difficult man for his immediate employees to get along with." If your narrator admired the mayor greatly, he will spring to his defense with an apt illustration of why your

statement is wrong. If he did find him hard to get along with, your remark has given him a chance to illustrate some of the mayor's more unpleasant characteristics.

12. Try to establish at every important point in the story where the narrator was or what his role was in this event, in order to indicate how much is eye-witness information and how much based on reports of others. "Where were you at the time of the mine disaster?" "Did you talk to any of the survivors later?" "Did their accounts differ in any way from the newspaper accounts of what happened?" Work around these questions carefully or you can appear to be doubting the accuracy of the narrator's account.

13. Do not challenge accounts you think may be inaccurate. Instead, try to develop as much information as possible that can be used by later researchers in establishing what probably happened. Your narrator may be telling you quite accurately what he saw. As Walter Lord explained when describing his interview with survivors of the *Titanic,* "Every lady I interviewed had left the sinking ship in the last lifeboat. As I later found out from studying the placement of the lifeboats, no group of lifeboats was in view of another and each lady probably *was* in the last lifeboat she could see leaving the ship."

14. Do tactfully point out to your narrator that there is a different account of what he is describing, if there is. Start out "I have heard . . ." or "I have read. . . ." This is not a challenge to his account, but rather an opportunity for him to bring up further evidence to refute the opposing view, or to explain how that view got established, or to temper what he has already said. If done skillfully, some of your best information can come from this juxtaposition of differing accounts.

15. Try to avoid "off the record" information— the times when your narrator asks you to turn off the recorder while he tells you a good story. Ask him to let you record the whole thing and promise

that you will erase that portion if he asks you to after further consideration. You may have to erase it later, or he may not tell you the story at all, but once you allow "off the record" stories, he may continue with more and more and you will end up with almost no recorded interview at all. "Off the record" information is only useful if you yourself are researching a subject and this is the only way you can get the information. It has no value if your purpose it to collect information for later use by other researchers.

16. Don't switch the recorder off and on. It is much better to waste a little tape on irrelevant material than to call attention to the tape recorder by a constant on-off operation. For this reason, I do not recommend the stop-start switches available on some mikes. If your mike has such a switch, tape it to "on" to avoid an inadvertent missing of material—then forget it. Of course you can turn off the recorder if the telephone rings or someone interrupts your session.

17. Interviews usually work out better if there is no one present except the narrator and the interviewer. Sometimes two or more narrators can be successfully recorded, but usually each one of them would have been better alone.

18. Do end the interview at a reasonable time. An hour and a half is probably maximum. First, you must protect your narrator against over-fatigue; second, you will be tired even if he isn't. Some narrators tell you very frankly if they are tired, or their wives will. Otherwise, you must plead fatigue, another appointment, or no more tape.

19. Don't use the interview to show off your own knowledge, vocabulary, charm, or other abilities. Good interviewers do not shine; only their interviews do.

Indexing

Tapes

It is most efficient to index the tape shortly after you return from the interview. Tapes can be indexed by time segments, such as five-minute intervals. While most tape recorders have an index counter, often called a digital counter, our experience is that these are not standard and that tape indexes prepared according to the count on one machine are not accurate on another machine, nor even on the same machine a year later. I therefore recommend a time-segment index. This can be prepared by listening through the tape, watching a clock, and writing down the major topic of discussion during each five- to ten-minute segment. For example:

00 Kringle family background, from Ohio.
07 Father's trip west in 1870.
12 Farming in Central County, wheat, pests, depression of 1890's.
20 College days at UC Berkeley, class of 1904. Professors, students, social life.
28 Return to Central City, marriage, job in Central City Bank.
34 Bank practices, 1905 to World War I.
   Second side of tape
00 World War I, France.
05 Banking in Central City, 1920's.
                    etc.

Include with the index, and file with the tape, a list of names (correctly spelled), dates, hard-to-hear phrases or old-fashioned phrases, and other information that will assist the researcher at a future time. A sample tape index sheet used for the Bancroft Library's Donated Tape Collection follows.

DONATED TAPES COLLECTION
REGIONAL ORAL HISTORY OFFICE

The Bancroft Library
University of California
Berkeley, California 94720

General Topic of Interview _____

Date _____ Place _____ Length _____

Personal Data:

Narrator	Interviewer
Name _____	Name _____
Address _____	Address _____
_____	_____
Name, address of relative, friend	Relationship to narrator (neighbor,
_____	co-worker, etc.) _____
Birthplace _____	_____
Birthdate _____	Length of acquaintance _____
Occupation(s) _____	
_____	What was the occasion of the in-
_____	terview? _____
	_____

Interview Data:

Side 1

Side 2

Estimated time
on tape:

Subjects covered, in approximate order (please
spell out names of persons and places mentioned).

_____   _____
_____   _____
_____   _____
_____   _____
_____   _____
_____   _____
_____   _____
_____   _____

Use back of sheet if necessary

Transcripts

If you transcribe, it is possible to prepare an alphabetical index of names and subjects. Index persons, places, and subjects, but only if there is some real information about them in the transcript. Do not index "Theodore Roosevelt" if the information is "I remember as a kid I saw Teddy Roosevelt as he came through town on a campaign trip. It was quite a thrill to wave at the President of the United States and I was sure he waved back." The historian looking up fresh information on Theodore Roosevelt will only be irritated to have spent the time to consult that tape. Good indexing requires some discrimination. A complete index may be as useless as it is impressive looking.

Interviews

Keep an index of your interviews by name of narrator, geographic area discussed, and by the major subjects covered in the interviews. This is the guide researchers will consult first. They may be looking up "banking" or "Central City." A quick look through the files will lead them to the Kringle interview, another look at the Kringle interview index will indicate whether it is worthwhile to listen to that tape or read that transcript. Most researchers have a limited amount of time to go through a vast amount of material; indexes of all sorts should be prepared with the object of guiding the researcher most rapidly to whatever he is searching for.

Making Information about Oral History Interviews Available to Researchers

The society's job of making oral history interviews available to researchers is not completed when the sought-for information has been captured on tape or transcript and has been indexed for easy use. The bottleneck has always been that persons doing research and writing have no means of knowing what rich resources on their topic might

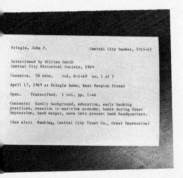

Kringle, John P.   Central City banker, 1913-65

Interviewed by William Smith
Central City Historical Society, 1969

Cassette, 50 mins.   vol. K-1-69 no. 1 of 3

April 17, 1969 at Kringle home, East Hampton Street

Open. Transcribed. 1 vol. pp. 1-46

Contents: family background, education, early banking practices, reaction to war-time economy, banks during Great Depression, bank merger, move into present bank headquarters.

(See also: Banking, Central City Trust Co., Great Depression)

exist in the oral history collections of historical societies or libraries. One modest way to publicize the existence of oral history materials is to exchange information with other similar historical materials centers, both those in the region (for regional historians) and those that emphasize the same subjects (i.e., agriculture, maritime history, crafts, etc.). This can be done by sending out lists of the oral history accessions for the year with a brief listing of subjects covered in each interview, and by requesting the other institutions to send their lists in return. Such lists can be kept on file and made available to researchers who come into the society. Most major oral history offices publish catalogs of their holdings and these should also be collected. The Oral History Association *Newsletter* is the best guide to such catalogs.

The California State Library has recently instituted a more systemized and mechanized method of collecting data on all oral history tapes and transcripts available in California. Libraries, historical societies, and museums have been asked to participate in the California Bibliographic Center for Oral History by sending to the state library a card on each interview they hold. The card lists person or persons interviewed, subjects covered, length of tape, whether or not a transcript is available, and where and under what circumstances the interview may be used by researchers. The data submitted is being edited to standard bibliographic form and converted to machine-readable form. In time the scholar of California history can discover this primary historical material available throughout the state by utilizing a central file at the state library. Local historical societies in other states can encourage their own state library or state historical society to launch a similar program.

Agreements on Use

A Pre-recording Understanding

It is wise to have written evidence of the narrator's understanding of the purpose and procedures of the program, and of his agreement to permit the use of his interviews for historical research. First, although you probably will have talked to him in person and will have explained the whole program, write him a letter explaining again why you are doing the recording, what the procedure will be, and make it clear that these tapes will be available for historical research. In the Bancroft Library we send the narrator two copies of this letter and ask him to sign one and return it to us if the plan as outlined meets his approval. You may not want to be that formal, but at least have on file a carbon of the letter you sent him.

The Agreement on Use

As soon as you have completed all of the recording, have the narrator sign an agreement on use. The simpler the agreement, the better. Many narrators are frightened by complex and legalistic releases.

Have the rights to use turned over to an organization that can be expected to exist for a long time, the historical society most likely; but if this is a temporary oral history program, the city or county library may be the most appropriate depository and owner.

The wording of a simple agreement for the Central City Historical Society is included here as a sample.

CENTRAL CITY HISTORICAL SOCIETY
85 MAIN STREET
CENTRAL CITY, MISSOURI

I hereby give and grant to the CENTRAL CITY HISTORICAL SOCIETY
as a donation for such scholarly and educational purposes as
the Society shall determine the tape recordings and their
contents listed below.

_____
Name of narrator

_____
Address of narrator

_____
Name of interviewer

_____
Address of interviewer

_____
Date of agreement

_____
Subject of Tape(s)

Ask Permission to Use a Substantial
Portion of the Interview

If it is planned to use any substantial portion of an interview in a public way, say, in a newspaper or a historical monument pamphlet, it is only common courtesy to ask the narrator for his permission before using it. He will probably be pleased. But if he doesn't want it used, no matter how generous he has been in signing over all rights to the society, *do not use it.* Nothing will damage an oral history program as much as a disgruntled narrator who feels his material has been used improperly.

Restricting Material

Very occasionally a narrator will divulge some information which he wishes "put under seal" (i.e., closed to all use) for a certain number of years, or which the interviewer feels should be put under seal. This can be handled in the signed agreement by a sentence added to the usual statement. This is the sentence used by the Bancroft Library:

> *Limitation on publication.* The parties hereto agree that pages 14-16 of the manuscript and the portions of the tape from which these pages were transcribed shall not be published or otherwise made available to anyone other than the parties hereto until January 1, 1984.

Work out with the narrator a reasonable time limitation based upon why he wishes it placed under seal. It may be "during the lifetime of the narrator" or a date when all the persons involved can be presumed to have died.

Alternatives other than "open" or "sealed" are "closed during the narrator's lifetime except with his permission," or "open only with the permission of the president of the society."

Our one experience with "closed during the narrator's lifetime except with his permission" was unfortunate. The narrator's purpose in placing the limitation had been that he personally wanted to

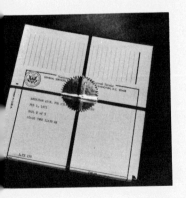

meet the scholars who were working on his topic, just for fun and because he felt he would surely be able to answer some of their questions specifically and in greater detail than he had in his interview. Alas, the narrator lived on for many years in a condition of poor health which made it impossible for him to grant permission; the interview was therefore closed until his death. Several Ph.D. theses were written during this time on subjects he had discussed, but none could incorporate his comments.

By all means avoid any transferring of discretion over use of the interview to heirs. Let the narrator make up his own mind on when to open the material.

Closed Is Closed

Whatever the agreement, it must be adhered to rigidly.

If the interview is to be put under seal, pack into a box the tape, the notes about the interview, and the tape index, tie it securely, seal it with wax, mark on the outside the date when it can be opened, and put it away in a safe place. A card indicating generally what the tape is about, but not specifically what the closed material is, can be kept in the society's oral history files. It should be marked "closed until 1980" or "closed until five years after Mr. A. B. Doe's death" or whatever the restriction is.

The interviewer, and the transcriber if the interview was transcribed, must also adhere to the agreement by not talking about the closed information. "I am sorry but Mr. Doe has closed his interview until 1980" should be the end of any conversation about it.

Discourage Restricted Material

In most instances the focus of the oral history program is such that there is no reason to collect material that must be closed. Except in the few cases where sensitive material is really pertinent, it should be discouraged. If interviews are not transcribed, a few closed sentences mean the whole tape becomes inaccessible for a period of time. If the material is transcribed, only the sensitive pages and the tape need to be sealed, the rest of the transcript can be open. However, this still necessitates a foolproof on-going system of keeping the material closed and then of opening it on the appointed date. The operation of an active oral history program will involve enough details without adding one more of such long duration.

Ethics of Oral History

The value and continuation of oral history interviewing depend upon the voluntary ethical conduct of oral history practitioners, and upon the ability of oral history projects to abide by their agreements over whatever period of time is stipulated.

Responsibility to the Narrator

It is the responsibility of the oral history practitioner to deal fairly in every respect. The value of the interviews that will be conducted with the narrator depends upon the confidence he has in the interviewer, in the reputation of the historical society, and in the reputation of the entire field of oral history. The members of an oral history project have the following responsibilities to the narrator:

1. To make clear to the narrator what the process will be at each step, how the material will be handled, and what restrictions he can place upon it.

2. To get down what happened as accurately as possible, and to this end to work together with the narrator to record the information. This will include developing delicate or controversial material (where relevant) in such a way as to give the narrator the fullest opportunity to record his point of view.

3. To advise him, with his interests in mind, as to what the best agreement on use would be. If, in your opinion, something he said could be used in a way damaging to him, advise him to put it under seal. It will be of no benefit to the oral history program to have a narrator's reputation damaged through something he said in an oral history interview.

4. To adhere to any agreements made.

Responsibility to the Historical Profession

Every effort should be made to maintain the good reputation of oral history as a field by keeping faith with the narrators. In addition, the oral history materials produced should be made as useful to researchers as possible. This includes:

1. Produce the best interviews you can.
2. Make a typescript, if at all possible.
3. Index the tapes or transcripts.
4. Make the existence of your oral history materials known.
5. Make it possible for researchers to use the materials (unless they are under seal).

Oral History Association Goals and Guidelines

The Oral History Association by unanimous approval adopted the following statement on November 25, 1968.

ORAL HISTORY ASSOCIATION
Goals and Guidelines

The Oral History Association recognizes Oral History for what it is—a method of gathering a body of historical information in oral form usually on tape. Because the scholarly community is involved in both the production and use of oral history, the Association recognizes an opportunity and an obligation on the part of all concerned to make this type of historical source as authentic and as useful as possible.

Guidelines for the Interviewee:

1. The person who is interviewed should be selected carefully and his wishes must govern the conduct of the interview.

2. Before undertaking a taped interview for the purpose stated above, the interviewee (or narrator) should be clear in his mind regarding mutual rights with respect to tapes and transcripts made from them. This includes such things as: seal privilege, literary rights, prior use, fiduciary relationships, the right to edit the tape transcriptions, and the right to determine whether the tape is to be disposed of or preserved.

3. It is important that the interviewee fully understand the project, and that in view of costs and effort involved he assumes a willingness to give useful information on the subject being pursued.

Guidelines for the Interviewer:

1. It should be the objective of the interviewer to gather information that will be of scholarly usefulness in the present and the future. The interviewer who is collecting oral history materials for his own individual research should always bear in mind his broader objective.

2. In order to obtain a tape of maximum worth as a historical document, it is incumbent upon the interviewer to be thoroughly grounded in the background and experiences of the person being interviewed, and, where appropriate and if at all feasible, to review the papers of the interviewee before conducting the interview. In

conducting the interview an effort should be made to provide enough information to the interviewee to assist his recall.

3. It is important that all interviews be conducted in a spirit of objectivity and scholarly integrity and in accordance with stipulations agreed upon.

Guidelines for Sponsoring Institutions:

1. Subject to meeting the conditions as prescribed by interviewees, it will be the obligation of sponsoring institutions to prepare easily usable tapes and/or accurate typed transcriptions, and properly to identify, index, and preserve such oral history records for use by the scholarly community, and to state clearly the provisions that govern their use.

Unanimously adopted by the Oral History Association, November 25, 1968

Members of the OHA "Goals And Guidelines Committee" that prepared preliminary versions of this statement and submitted a draft to the members at the Nebraska meeting for further discussion and revision were Oscar Winther (Chairman) of Indiana University; Professor James Harvey Young of Emory University; Dr. Philip C. Brooks, Director of the Harry S. Truman Library in Independence, Missouri; and Mrs. Amelia Fry of the Regional Oral History Office at the University of California at Berkeley.

Approval of this statement concluded a two-year effort to formulate a position paper about the general concerns of oral historians.

Legal Restrictions

There are few legal restrictions that limit the collection and publication of historical materials. Slander or libel are the ones most likely to be of concern to oral historians. Slander is the oral or written defamation of a person by means of a false report, maliciously uttered, which injures the reputation of the person. Libel is defamation by the publication of this kind of false utterance, without just cause, and which tends to expose the other to public hatred, contempt, or ridicule.

Various court cases have progressively reduced the possibility of a court finding any historical effort either slanderous or libelous. First, the dead cannot be libeled. Second, libelous defamation of prominent living persons must include actual malice plus irresponsible disregard for the truth.

The researcher or interviewer may need to be a little more concerned if his questioning leads him into the purely private lives of prominent or not-prominent persons, although he still has a good defense if he can indicate this is truth published for good motives. Of course, there always exists the possibility of harassment in the lower courts through filing of suits for defamation. Such suits stand almost no possibility of ending in court award for damages but they could cost time and expense to the researcher in defending himself. But to all intents and purposes, slander or libel is a non-existent danger to an oral history project. It is the project's reputation for responsible work that needs guarding, not its legal liability.

The question of literary property rights is a little more complicated and court cases have not been numerous enough nor one-directional enough to serve as guides to oral historians. Congress is presently holding hearings on what promises to be a substantial revision of all previous copyright laws. Therefore, the best advice is to get a proper signed release for use of all interviews, and then to go to the added courtesy of getting specific permission for publication of any substantial portions. It is better to err on the side of asking for too many permissions than to damage the good public relations of the society.

Deposit and Preservation of Tapes

Where to Deposit Tapes

Two considerations should govern where you deposit the tapes:

1. Long-term safety and preservation
2. Accessibility for research

If the historical society has a relatively fireproof building or permanent location, if its library or museum is open on a regular basis for a reasonable number of hours weekly, and if the society seems to be a permanent organization able to meet long-term commitments, then by all means keep the tapes and other related manuscripts right there. If, however, the society's office is in the living room of the current president, or, while it has a permanent building, it is open only two afternoons a week, then consider the local library as a more available place in which to deposit the tapes and manuscripts for use by the public. In a smaller community, it would be logical for the historical society and the library to share the responsibility of working on local history, the society collecting papers, producing oral history interviews, and managing the museum or historic sites; the library preserving and servicing the manuscript and oral history materials.

Sometimes it is suggested that in order to facilitate research, the oral history interviews should be deposited in a central depository such as the state historical society or a university or state library. Assuming that the interview material is primarily local in nature, it would seem more important for the researcher to work right in the community in order to use other papers there and to get the feel of the area. The prime users will probably be persons from the community itself, who would find travel to an out-of-town depository an inconvenience.

Collecting Other Materials

The value of the oral history information will be enhanced if you can collect other illustrative ma-

terials. The narrator may have letters, clippings, reports, photographs, printed programs, or other items which would be useful to the researcher. These should be collected if possible and filed with the tapes, or in separate files but cross-catalogued. Try to get a photograph of the narrator at the time of the interview, even if you have to take along your own camera to do it.

Storage and Handling of Tapes

1. Store tapes under "people conditions." Ideal "people conditions" are ideal tape use and storage conditions. In broad terms this means a fairly constant temperature in the 70's, and a relative humidity of about 50 percent. If the tapes are subjected to extreme cold or heat, do not listen to them until they have had at least twenty-four hours to stabilize at good "people conditions." Do not use artificial means to hasten this stabilization period.

2. Handle in a "clean-room" environment. Dust and lint can damage tapes when they are used, so try to approach a "clean-room" environment in the listening area. Do not eat, drink, or smoke where tapes are handled. Smoke will not damage the tapes but fine ashes will. Avoid getting fingerprints on the tapes and do not use a grease or wax pencil to mark them; these will only attract and hold dust particles.

3. Store in the original box. Tapes should be stored in the cardboard or plastic containers they came in, *standing on edge* on a shelf. The containers can be placed in a pastic bag for additional protection against dust and moisture.

4. Wind tape evenly, rewind occasionally. Of primary importance is the way the tape is wound on the reel, as poor winding can result in distortion of the tape. This should be a firm, stable wind, not pulled taut nor so loose as to allow some strands to wrinkle. All the edges should be even, not some protruding above the others. Before putting a tape away for storage, rewind it from beginning to end to assure uniform tension. Occasionally rewinding

a tape (every six months to a year) or playing it will relieve strains and adhesions before they seriously affect the tape.

5. Protect tape reels. When handling reels, pick them up by the hub, not the flanges. Check all empty tape reels before reusing them. Do not use those that look warped or damaged in any way.

6. Snip end of tape which has become damaged.

7. Do not use clear cellophane mending tapes to affix anything to the reels of tape or the insides of the containers.

8. Avoid stray magnetic fields. Avoid accidental exposure to magnetic fields from electric generators or motors as this can lead to print-through or complete erasure. Do not store tapes near a steady field of DC current, a permanent magnet, or a concentrated field of AC current. And avoid magnetic catches on the cupboards in the tape storage room.

9. Clean tape recorder periodically.

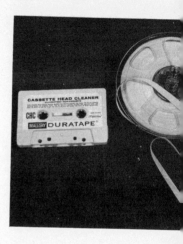

Allowing Persons to Use the Tapes

Do not permit tapes to be taken out of the depository for listening or other uses unless you retain the original tape and have a copy that can be lent out. You should have a tape recorder and earphones available in the depository for persons to use for listening. The recorder should be kept clean so the tapes will not be damaged.

Of course it is possible to erase a tape by pushing the "record" button. Most recorders have a "record lock" which must be pushed at the same time as the "record" button, so that it takes two fingers, which is some protection against accidental erasure. However, if the recorder in the depository is to be used chiefly for listening to tapes, it would be wise to have an electronics repairman prepare a semi-permanent lock on the "record" button. When this is screwed into place, the user cannot erase a tape. This arrangement would not interfere with using the recorder for transcribing. (It could also be used by libraries which make musical tapes available to their patrons.)

To Transcribe or Not to Transcribe

Much can be said for transcribing and much against it. Each historical society will have to weigh the pros and cons and then make its own decision on whether or not to transcribe.

For Transcribing

1. The transcribed interview, corrected by the interviewer and the narrator and indexed by names and subjects, is much easier for researchers to use than an audio tape. A researcher can skim through a transcript faster than he can listen, even selectively, to a tape. The transcript will therefore get more use.

2. A corrected transcript may be more accurate and complete because the recorded words were put down in writing while the narrator was still available to clear up obscurities. Words that are hard to hear can be checked by the actual speaker, questions that were inadequately answered can be expanded by written comment.

3. The historical society will have something visible to show for its effort. A copy for the narrator is a rich reward for his participation in the project.

Against Transcribing

1. Time and cost. Some special equipment will be needed. The historical society can expect to expend an average of six to twelve typing hours for each hour of recording. This will result in a rough transcript; in order to look nice and be most easily used it should be retyped after it has been corrected. It should be indexed. All these steps are as time-consuming as they are useful.

2. If you transcribe you must give a copy of the interview to the narrator for his corrections. This will require further negotiations. He may insist on rewriting the whole thing. If you do not transcribe, after you have completed the recordings and your

brief index of what is on the tape, the job is finished. If you transcribe, you are less than half-way through after you have done the recording.

My personal recommendation—remembering that there are those who disagree—is that the historical society start with the intention of recording only, but that as the program becomes better established, and if there are typists on the oral history committee, a cautious beginning be made at transcribing some of the best tapes. A well-organized program with sufficient skilled volunteers can handle transcribing, and the results will be well worth the effort. However, at no time should the tape-recording program be allowed to bog down because of the complexities of the transcribing steps. First things first.

Transcribing Equipment

Efficient, speedy transcribing requires that the transcribing machine have a full-function foot-pedal (stop/start and reverse) so that the typist can work without removing her hands from the typewriter. There are few such machines available.

Tape recorders that come with a remote stop/start microphone can be fitted with a stop/start foot-pedal, but not with reverse. Several cassette recorders have back-space review buttons which, although operated by hand, make those machines fairly convenient for transcribing.

Full-Function Transcribing Machines

Reel-to-reel:

TANDBERG, Model 1521 F, 23 pounds, takes 7-inch reels, 3 speeds. The favorite of most oral history offices. Can also make excellent recordings in the office. $400.

UHER 5000, 16 pounds, 5-inch reels only, 3 speeds but not $7\frac{1}{2}$. $500.

Cassette:

CRAIG 2702. A basic transcribing machine. $190.

WOLLENSAK 2540 AV. For dictation. With foot control A-0542, total cost is $340.

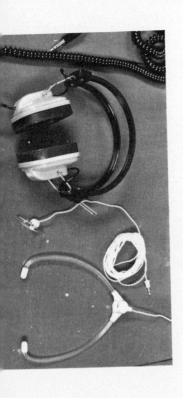

DICTAPHONE 241. Many extras available for convenient dictating. Recommended for C-60s only. Our machine tangles and breaks C-90s. $450.

While these transcribing tape recorders can also record, they are not designed to be carried about as portable units. The most efficient set-up is to have two tape recorders, one a small portable for interviews, the other a transcribing machine which remains in the office.

A good pair of headphones, ranging in cost from $12 to $25 (mono, not stereo) will help in hearing, and will permit the transcriber to work without bothering other people in the same room.

Transcribing Time

It takes an average of six to twelve hours to transcribe a one-hour tape. This will vary a great deal depending on the speaker and the acoustical conditions of the tape, and, of course, the skill of the transcriber. Much background noise, a person who speaks with a foreign accent, a complicated subject, a machine-gun delivery, a narrator who has suffered a stroke—any of these, for example, may increase the transcribing time up to fifteen hours per hour of tape.

Who Should Transcribe

Transcribing is a challenging, interesting task that requires more than average secretarial abilities. Good typing is less essential than a sharp mind. The transcriber should have a broad general background, be able to spell, and know how to punctuate so as to catch the meaning of the spoken word. Improper punctuation can completely change the meaning of a series of words. The transcriber must have the discrimination to determine from the context which word to type when several words sound similar, when to leave in an uncompleted sentence because it is important and when to leave it out because the narrator just made a false start, when to include editorial remarks such as "(sarcastic laughter)." A keen ear for electronic sound is essential; some people just can't hear the sound from a tape recorder.

Method of Transcribing

Transcribe almost verbatim, but listen ahead sufficiently to leave out false starts, fumbling for the correct word, coffee-time conversation unless it is pertinent, or too many "you know's" or "well's." Retain the speech characteristics of the narrator, but do not try to spell out phonetically unusual pronunciations such as "yup" for "yes." Do not improve grammar or word order.

In the interest of an uninterrupted narrative, some transcribers try to eliminate the interviewer's questions. This gives a false picture of why the narrator said what he said. Retain the questions.

Leave a blank for unintelligible portions, noting down in pencil the approximate point on the tape where this occurred. The interviewer will probably be able to listen through and catch it. Try to approximate the spelling of spoken names; again, the interviewer may be able to correct them. Ideally, the interviewer will take notes of all names mentioned during the interview and will have the narrator check these for correct spelling.

Prepare three copies of the transcript, one to keep verbatim, one to use for editing and correcting by the interviewer as a working copy, and one to prepare neatly and submit to the narrator for his final corrections. If you do not intend to retype the corrected copy, you will want to use one copy for the society's files and have one copy for the narrator to keep.

Submitting the Transcript to the Narrator for His Review

Do not return portions of the transcript to the narrator until the entire interview has been tape-recorded. If you return the transcript to him week by week, you will find much time is spent in revising or re-recording rather than in getting on with the story. After all of the recording is completed, the transcript can be submitted chapter by chapter (if the series was long, asking someone to correct several hundred pages would be too overwhelming), or in entirety if the manuscript is of manageable size for the narrator.

Ask the narrator to read the transcript carefully, correcting errors of fact or spelling, but *urge him not* to try to formalize the conversational style. Reiterate again and again, in person and by letter, that you want this to read as a conversation, that you want to retain the spontaneity of the spoken word. You may have to speak to his spouse as well, and you may be well advised to stop by his house to see what he is doing with the transcript if he keeps it too long. Many narrators, especially of the older generation, find it almost impossible to resist revising their transcripts into what they think would have been an acceptable essay for their high school English teacher.

Encouraging the Use of Oral History Materials

Stimulate Use

So far we have been discussing the first and major role of the oral history committee, that of getting information onto tape and then of indexing it and making it available for use. A second responsibility is to try to get the tapes or transcripts into use now. It is only through feed-back from users that the committee has any way to measure the value of the interviews. Having the material used will please the narrators (if it doesn't, don't use it yet), publicize the program, and raise the morale of the oral history committee. So do put some effort into finding ways to use the material soon. Some possible immediate uses follow.

Historical Research

The primary use, of course, is for historical research, and most of this will be in the future. It will be many years before you know how well this has worked out. Of one thing you may be certain, no user will be satisfied with your interviews; each will wish you had spent more time on the subject of his special concern and had not wasted your time on subjects he is not interested in. In trying to out-guess the future, aim at a well-rounded interview with emphasis on what the narrator can tell best.

However, many interviews will fit in with the current research interests of members of the historical society. By all means encourage local researchers to participate in the interviewing, have them submit questions to be asked that will provide information for their research, and publicize what interviews you have so that researchers will come and use them.

Newspaper Columns on Local History

Several local historical societies report that the newspaper runs excerpts from their oral history interviews, often on some timely theme. (For example, the opening of a new school may be the occasion for several columns on the early schools of the vicinity.) They report that a local-history column is especially popular with newcomers to the area. Oral history has much to offer to the many wandering Americans who attempt to sink roots into a new community.

Narrative for Slide Lectures

Well-edited excerpts from a number of interviews can provide a taped narrative for a series of slides, making a lively lecture on local history for schools or organizations.

Taped Descriptions for Museum Exhibits

Very brief excerpts, less than one minute, can be prepared as push-button descriptions of exhibits. How much more interesting to hear an actual user of an antiquated implement explaining what he did with it than to read the description on the wall.

Classroom Use

Various illustrated lectures with taped excerpts can be prepared to interest different age levels. However, a more effective use of oral history is to locate especially cooperative and stimulating narrators, then have the children prepare questions and go out and record them themselves. The preparation of the questions, the recording session, and then the presentation of the results to the class can be an invaluable experience.

Developing Expertise

Successful oral history program planning and interviewing is a skill that comes only from experience plus careful evaluation of the work that has been completed. You learn by doing, so the first step is to start doing.

Interviews—Analyze Your Own Tapes

Your first listen-through of a completed tape will be to prepare the tape index and notes and to jot down questions for the next interviewing session. Later, listen through again, this time for the sole purpose of listing questions, comments, or procedures that went well, and those that went badly. For example, "How did you feel about that?" may have gotten a good response, while "You don't say!" may have shut him up completely. Switching off the machine while you asked him to pass the sugar and cream for your coffee and then switching it on again may have formalized an easy-rolling story. Assume that you are to use this tape to instruct some novices in what to do and what not to do. Here, as in asking questions about people, the negative approach is often more fruitful than the positive. While it is very hard to illustrate what to do, it is easy to see what not to do.

Committee Workshops

When several persons have completed tapes, plan a workshop for just the oral history committee, or maybe for only three or four interviewers on the committee. Have each participant bring in one or two examples of errors. They may also be asked to bring in an example of a successful way out of a problem, but those are harder to illustrate (and less fun for the committee).

I recall a period in my high school years when we vied with each other in reporting our "boners." These were gross ineptitudes in handling social problems—the wrong thing said at a given moment,

the stumble as one tried to make a graceful exit—
and as poiseless adolescents we had plenty to report each day. It was a bit cheering as one found
oneself in a mortifying situation to think about what
a funny story it would make at the next "boner"
session.

In this same spirit, if the emphasis at workshops
can be kept on a rather jocular confession of one's
own errors, with the group mulling over what might
have been done in the situation, it can be very
useful, enjoyable, and without damage to people's
feelings.

Regional or State Workshops

Many questions of mutual interest, which will
arise among historical societies conducting oral history programs, can be very usefully discussed at
meetings attended by representatives of a number
of societies. The workshop could be on oral history
in general, or it could be focused on any one of the
considerations mentioned in this booklet. Persons
charged with various responsibilities in the oral history program could participate in the section on
their specialty.

The Oral History Association

In 1967 a national association was formed of persons interested or engaged in oral history. The
Oral History Association holds an annual colloquium
in various sections of the United States. These are
intensive three-day workshops of panels, lectures,
discussion groups, and demonstrations on the many
phases of oral history. The discussions are published
in the Oral History Association *Proceedings* and
the *Oral History Review*. The Oral History Association also publishes quarterly the *OHA Newsletter*, which reports on oral history developments;
a *Directory, Oral History in the United States;* and
a *Bibliography on Oral History*. Members receive
current publications and can order back publications at a reduced price. This is a best buy for any
group practicing oral history. Write Oral History
Association, Waterman Building, University of Vermont, Burlington, Vermont 05401.

Bibliography

This is a selected bibliography of articles that have the most bearing on oral history for the volunteer historical society. See *Bibliography on Oral History*, Oral History Association, for more references.

Oral History in General

Tyrrell, William G. *Tape Recording Local History,* Technical Leaflet 35, American Association for State and Local History. May, 1966, 12 pp. Available for 50¢ from the Association, 1315 Eighth Avenue South, Nashville, Tennessee 37203. This leaflet should be your first acquisition for your oral history library.

A Guide for Oral History Programs, 1973. Instructions and samples on every step of the oral history process from funding to cataloguing; and *An Oral History Primer* by Gary L. Shumway and William G. Hartley, 1973, on interviewing and finishing the transcript, both available from the Oral History Program, California State University, Fullerton, California 92631.

Oral History Society (England) publishes a journal, *Oral History,* that contains many useful articles on interviewing. Especially relevant is *Oral History, No. 4: The Interview in Social History.* £1—about $2.50. Publications and membership (£3 a year, about $7.50), Dr. Paul Thompson, Department of Sociology, University of Essex, Colchester CO4 3SQ, England.

Hoyle, Norman. "Oral History," in *Library Trends* (July 1972), pp. 60-81.

Starr, Louis M. "Oral History: Problems and Prospects," in *Advances in Librarianship,* Vol. 2, edited by Melvin J. Voight, 1971.

American Archivist, XXVIII (January, 1965), 53-83. Four articles dealing with the problems and procedures of the professional oral history projects of the Harry Truman Library, a National Science Foundation project, Columbia University, and the Cornell University Program in Oral History.

Wilson Library Bulletin, XL (March, 1966), 600-28. Almost the entire issue is devoted to articles on oral history, all from the point of view of the large institution.

Oral History Interviewing Methods

Baum, Willa Klug. "Oral History: A Revived Tradition of the Bancroft Library," *Pacific Northwest Quarterly*, LVIII (April, 1967), 57-64.

Fry, Amelia R. "The Nine Commandments of Oral History," *Journal of Library History*, III (January, 1968), 63-73. A satire on the do's and don'ts of interviewing.

Gilb, Corinne L. "Tape-Recorded Interviewing: Some Thoughts from California," *American Archivist*, XX (October, 1957), 335-44.

White, Helen McCann. "Thoughts on Oral History," *American Archivist*, XX (January, 1957), 19-30. One of the earlier how-to-do-it articles.

Uses of Oral History

Morrissey, Charles T. "Oral History and the Mythmakers," *Historic Preservation*, XVI (1964), and "Oral History as a Classroom Tool," *Social Education*, XXXII (October, 1968), 546-49.

Lieber, Joel. "The Tape Recorder as Historian," *Saturday Review*, June 11, 1966.

Starr, Louis M. "History, Warm," *Columbia University Forum*, V (Fall, 1962), 27-30.

Legal Problems

Kelly, Alfred H. "Constitutional Liberty and the Law of Libel," *American Historical Review*, LXXIV (December, 1968), pp. 429-52.

Care of Tapes

Recording Basics. Magnetic Products Division, 3M Company. St. Paul, Minnesota 55101. $1.

"Magnetic Tape Erasure—How Serious the Threat?" 3M Company. Free.

"Tips on Tape Storage." 3M Company. Free.

Understanding High Fidelity. Pioneer Electronics Corporation, 178 Commerce Road, Carstadt, New Jersey 07072. Free.

Published Books Based on Oral History

Blyth, Ronald. *Akenfield: Portrait of an English Village.* New York: Grove Press, 1969.

Bullock, Paul. *Watts, the Aftermath.* New York: Grove Press, 1969.

Evans, George Ewart. *Where Beards Wag All: The Relevance of the Oral Tradition.* London: Faber & Faber, 1970.

Foxfire, Volumes I and II, edited by Eliot Wiggington. New York: Doubleday, 1972 and 1973.

Joseph, Peter. *Good Times: An Oral History of America in the 1960s.* New York: Charterhouse, 1973.

Myers, John M. *The Westerners.* New Jersey: Prentice-Hall, 1969.

Seidenbaum, Art. *Confrontation on Campus—Student Challenge in California.* Los Angeles: Ward-Ritchie Press, 1969.

Terkel, Studs. *Hard Times: An Oral History of the Great Depression.* New York: Pantheon Books, 1970.

Williams, T. Harry. *Huey Long.* New York: Alfred A. Knopf, 1969.

American Association for State and Local History
1400 Eighth Avenue South
Nashville, Tennessee 37203

3 5282 00059 9285